Table of Contents

Reynolds Quick & Easy Packet Cooking

A simple, no-mess way to make delicious homecooked meals.

When you wrap food in Reynolds Wrap® Heavy Duty Aluminum Foil packets and then oven bake or grill it, the ingredients cook evenly and quickly, *and* there's no cleanup! Packet cooking also lets you customize your meals to suit the individual tastes in your family—if someone doesn't like an ingredient, such as pepper or onions, just leave that ingredient out of their foil packet. And for the family eating at different times, make up individual meals in foil packets and refrigerate. Packets can be baked in the oven one at a time or up to four at once as family schedules permit.

1. CENTER ingredients on a sheet (12×18 inches) of Reynolds Wrap Heavy Duty Aluminum Foil.

2. BRING up foil sides. Double fold top and ends to seal packet, leaving room for heat circulation inside. Repeat to make four packets.

3. BAKE on a cookie sheet in preheated 450°F oven, OR GRILL on medium-high in covered grill.

4. AFTER COOKING, open end of foil packet first to allow steam to escape. Then open top of foil packet.

No Soaking! No Scrubbing! No Kidding!

Line pans with Reynolds Wrap® Heavy Duty Aluminum Foil before you cook to avoid scrubbing afterwards.

● How To: Pan Lining

1. TURN pan upside down and press a sheet of foil around it.

2. REMOVE foil, flip pan over and drop foil inside.

3. CRIMP the edges and you're ready to cook!

When using Release® Non-Stick Foil, follow the above directions making sure that the non-stick (dull) side is facing down toward the pan when pressing foil around the pan. The non-stick side of the foil liner will be facing up toward the food when dropped inside the pan.

Reynolds Foil Makes Grilling Easy!

Use Reynolds Wrap® Heavy Duty Aluminum Foil for everyday grilling.

Use Reynolds Wrap® Release® Non-Stick Foil for your stickiest foods like barbecue chicken or ribs, marinated/glazed meat or fish and hard-to-grill veggies like asparagus, peppers and zucchini.

Stop BBQ Chicken from Sticking

Just line the grill grates with Reynolds Wrap® Release® Non-Stick Foil. Use a grilling fork to punch holes for drainage before placing the foil on the preheated grill. Moist, juicy chicken will lift right off, barbecue sauce and all.

Keep Shrimp and Veggies in Place

Keep small foods like shrimp and veggies from falling through the grill grate by lining it with Release® Non-Stick Foil. Lining the grate with non-stick foil prevents cleanup too. Be sure to punch a few holes for drainage and heat circulation.

DIY Foil Grill Pan

To make a Reynolds Foil Do-It-Yourself (DIY) Grill Pan, stack two sheets of Reynolds Wrap® Heavy Duty Aluminum Foil. Flip a 13×9×2-inch pan upside down. Press sheets of foil around pan. Remove foil from pan and crimp ends to form a rim. Place DIY Grill Pan on a tray to transport to and from the grill.

Asian Peach Glazed Ribs

Prep Time: 10 minutes ● **Grill Time:** 1 hour

- **2** sheets (18×24 inches *each*) Reynolds Wrap® Heavy Duty Aluminum Foil
- **3** pounds baby back pork ribs
- **½** cup water, divided

SEASONING RUB

- **1** tablespoon packed brown sugar
- **1** teaspoon 5-spice powder OR ground ginger
- **1** teaspoon celery salt
- **½** teaspoon paprika
- **¼** teaspoon ground red pepper

GLAZE

- **⅔** cup peach preserves
- **2** teaspoons fresh lemon juice
- **1** teaspoon soy sauce

PREHEAT grill to medium. Cut each rack of ribs into thirds. Center half of ribs in single layer on each sheet of Reynolds Wrap Heavy Duty Aluminum Foil.

COMBINE all Seasoning Rub ingredients. Sprinkle and rub seasoning over ribs, turning to coat evenly.

BRING up foil sides. Double fold top and one end. Through open end, pour in ¼ cup water. Double fold remaining end to seal packet, leaving room for heat circulation inside. Repeat to make two packets.

GRILL 45 minutes to 1 hour in covered grill. Remove ribs from foil; place on grill.

COMBINE peach preserves, lemon juice and soy sauce. Brush ribs generously with Glaze. **CONTINUE GRILLING** 10 to 15 minutes in uncovered grill, brushing with Glaze and turning every 5 minutes. Discard Glaze.

Makes 5 to 6 servings

REYNOLDS KITCHENS TIP:

Three or four ice cubes may be substituted for the water in each packet of ribs, if desired.

Grilled Fruit & Pound Cake

Prep Time: 15 minutes ● **Grill Time:** 4 minutes

Reynolds Wrap® Release® Non-Stick Foil

- ½ cup honey
- ¼ cup butter, melted
- ½ teaspoon ground cinnamon
- 8 slices pound cake, ½-inch thick
- 4 fresh peaches, peeled and halved
- 4 fresh pineapple slices, ½-inch thick
- 2 fresh bananas, quartered
   Fresh strawberries, hulled and halved
- 1 jar (11.75 ounces) hot fudge ice cream topping, heated

COMBINE honey, butter and cinnamon; set aside.

PREHEAT grill to medium-high. Make drainage holes in a sheet of Reynolds Wrap Release Non-Stick Foil with a large grilling fork.

BRUSH one side of cake slices with honey mixture.

PLACE foil sheet with holes on grill grate with non-stick (dull) side toward food. Immediately arrange cake slices brushed-side down on foil. **GRILL** 2 minutes in covered grill. Brush tops with honey mixture; turn. Grill 2 minutes longer or until lightly browned. Remove cake from foil.

BRUSH one side of peaches, pineapple and bananas with honey mixture; arrange brushed-side down, on foil. **GRILL** 4 minutes in covered grill. Brush tops with honey mixture; turn. Grill 3 to 4 minutes longer or until lightly browned. **REMOVE** fruit from foil. Garnish with strawberries; drizzle with hot fudge topping before serving.

Makes 4 servings

Grilled Cheesy Chicken Nachos

Prep Time: 8 minutes ● **Grill Time:** 5 minutes

Reynolds Wrap® Release® Non-Stick Aluminum Foil
- 4 cups (about 4 ounces) tortilla chips
- 2 cups Mexican style shredded cheese, divided
- 1 cup shredded, cooked chicken
- 1 cup salsa
- 1 small tomato, chopped
- ½ cup sliced black olives
- 2 green onions, sliced

PREHEAT grill to medium-high indirect heat. For indirect heat, the heat source (coals or gas burner) is on one side of grill. Make a Reynolds Do-It-Yourself (DIY) Grill Pan (to make a pan, see tip on page 5); place on a tray.

ARRANGE tortilla chips in an even layer in DIY Grill Pan. Sprinkle 1¾ cups cheese over tortilla chips.

COMBINE chicken and salsa; spoon over chips and cheese. Top with tomato, black olives and green onions. Sprinkle with remaining ¼ cup cheese. Slide pan onto grill grate.

GRILL 5 to 7 minutes or until cheese melts over indirect heat (the side of grill with no coals or flame underneath).

Makes 6 to 8 servings

Grilled Marinated Vegetables

Prep Time: 24 minutes ● **Grill Time:** 8 minutes

Reynolds Wrap® Release® Non-Stick Aluminum Foil

1   small green bell pepper, cut into thin strips

1   small red or yellow bell pepper, cut into thin strips

1   small red onion, thinly sliced

1   package (8 ounces) fresh baby portobello mushrooms, halved

2   tablespoons chopped fresh basil OR 1 tablespoon chopped fresh rosemary

3   tablespoons balsamic vinegar

2   tablespoons olive oil

2   cloves garlic, minced

   Salt and black pepper to taste

PREHEAT grill to medium-high.

COMBINE vegetables, basil, vinegar, oil, garlic, salt and black pepper in a large bowl. Cover with Reynolds® Plastic Wrap and marinate at room temperature 15 to 20 minutes. Place vegetables in an even layer in a Reynolds Foil Do-It-Yourself (DIY) Grill Pan (to make a pan, see tip on page 5). Slide pan onto grill grate.

GRILL 8 to 10 minutes in covered grill, turning frequently, until vegetables are crisp-tender. Slide foil pan from grill onto a cookie sheet to transport from the grill.

Makes 4 servings

Cauliflower with Fiery Cheese Sauce Packet

Prep Time: 5 minutes ● **Grill Time:** 8 minutes

- **1**   **sheet (18×24 inches) Reynolds Wrap® Heavy Duty Aluminum Foil**
- **4**   **cups cauliflower florets**
- **½**   **(8-ounce) jar pasteurized process cheese sauce**
- **1**   **teaspoon hot pepper sauce**
- **¼**   **teaspoon crushed red pepper flakes (optional)**

PREHEAT grill to medium-high.

CENTER cauliflower on sheet of Reynolds Wrap Heavy Duty Aluminum Foil. Combine cheese sauce, hot pepper sauce and red pepper flakes in medium bowl. Spoon sauce mixture over cauliflower.

BRING up foil sides. Double fold top and ends to seal making one large foil packet, leaving room for heat circulation inside.

GRILL 8 to 10 minutes in covered grill.

Makes 4 servings

Ginger Lime Teriyaki Glazed Chicken

Prep Time: 15 minutes • **Grill Time:** 22 minutes

Reynolds Wrap® Release® Non-Stick Foil
- 6 bone-in chicken pieces
- 1¾ cups soy sauce
- 1 teaspoon finely grated lime peel
- ½ cup fresh lime juice
- 3 cloves garlic, peeled, flattened with a knife
- 2 scallions, thinly sliced, white and green parts separated
- 1 (3-inch) piece fresh ginger, peeled, thinly sliced
- 2 tablespoons honey
- 1⅓ cups sugar
- 2 tablespoons sesame oil
- 1 tablespoon toasted sesame seeds

COMBINE soy sauce, lime peel, lime juice, garlic, scallion whites, ginger and honey in heavy saucepan; stir until honey is dissolved. Spoon half of marinade over chicken in baking dish. Cover with foil; refrigerate 1 hour, turning twice. Make drainage holes in sheet of Reynolds Wrap Release Non-Stick Foil with large grilling fork; set aside.

FOR GLAZE, add sugar to remaining marinade. Heat to boiling on medium-high. Reduce heat to medium; cook and stir occasionally about 10 minutes or until thick and syrupy. Strain glaze; let cool, glaze will thicken. Reserve ½ cup glaze for serving.

PREHEAT grill to medium-high. Place foil sheet with holes on grill with non-stick (dull) side toward food. Drain chicken; discard marinade. Brush sesame oil on both sides of chicken; place skin-side down on foil.

GRILL chicken 5 minutes each side. Brush both sides with glaze. **CONTINUE GRILLING** and basting 6 to 8 minutes longer per side or until skin is dark golden brown, chicken is tender and juices run clear or meat thermometer reads 170°F for breasts, 180°F for other pieces. If chicken browns too much, reduce heat to medium. Discard remaining basting glaze.

REMOVE chicken from foil. Drizzle with reserved glaze; sprinkle with scallion greens and sesame seeds.

Makes 4 to 6 servings

Grill Roasted Potato Salad

Prep Time: 15 minutes ● **Grill Time:** 12 minutes

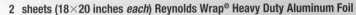

2   sheets (18×20 inches *each*) Reynolds Wrap® Heavy Duty Aluminum Foil

6   medium red potatoes, cut into 1-inch cubes

2   medium red or green bell peppers, cut into thin strips

1   package (12 ounces) fresh mushrooms, cut in half

3   tablespoons olive oil

4   cloves garlic, minced

2   teaspoons chopped fresh OR 1 teaspoon dried rosemary

    Salt and pepper to taste

1   package (8 ounces) or 6 cups torn mixed fresh salad greens

    Balsamic or wine vinegar

PREHEAT grill to medium-high. Make a Reynolds Do-It-Yourself (DIY) Non-Stick Foil Grill Pan (to make a pan, see tip on page 5); place on a tray.

COVER potato cubes with water in large saucepan. Bring to a boil; cook 5 minutes. Drain well. Toss potatoes, pepper strips, mushrooms, oil, garlic, rosemary, salt and pepper in large bowl until well coated. Spread mixture in DIY Grill Pan. Slide foil pan onto grill grate.

GRILL 12 to 15 minutes or until crisped and browned on medium-high in covered grill, stirring frequently. Slide foil pan from grill onto tray. Toss vegetables with salad greens and vinegar.

Makes 4 servings

Grilled Pineapple Curry Chicken

Prep Time: 20 minutes ● **Grill Time:** 13 minutes

Reynolds Wrap® Release®
Non-Stick Foil

CURRY RUB
- 2 tablespoons curry powder
- 2 teaspoons kosher salt
- 2 teaspoons black pepper
- 1 teaspoon packed brown sugar

COCONUT LIME SAUCE
- ½ cup coconut milk
- 1 teaspoon Curry Rub
  Juice from ½ fresh lime

HONEY BARBECUE SAUCE
- ¼ cup of your favorite barbecue sauce
- ¼ cup honey

INGREDIENTS
- 4 (4 to 6 ounces *each*) skinless, boneless chicken breast halves
- 1 medium red onion, sliced ¼-inch thick
- 1 tablespoon vegetable oil
- ½ medium fresh pineapple, cored and sliced ¼-inch thick

PREHEAT grill to medium-high. Make drainage holes in sheet of Reynolds Wrap Release Non-Stick Foil with large grilling fork; set aside.

COMBINE ingredients for Curry Rub, Coconut Lime Sauce and Honey Barbecue Sauce in separate bowls; set aside. Sprinkle remaining Curry Rub over chicken. Brush onion slices with oil.

PLACE foil sheet with holes on grill grate with non-stick (dull) side toward food; immediately place chicken, onion slices and pineapple slices on foil.

GRILL chicken, onion and pineapple 3 to 5 minutes; turn. Brush chicken and onion slices with Honey Barbecue Sauce; grill 5 minutes longer. Remove pineapple and onion slices from foil. Turn chicken and brush with barbecue sauce.
CONTINUE GRILLING 3 to 5 minutes or until chicken is tender or meat thermometer reads 170°F. Discard sauce. Place onion and pineapple slices on top of chicken. Drizzle with Coconut Lime Sauce. Grill 2 to 3 minutes or until sauce is heated.

Makes 4 servings

Honey Dijon Salmon Packets

Prep Time: 10 minutes ● **Grill Time:** 9 minutes

- **4** sheets (12×18 inches *each*) Reynolds Wrap® Heavy Duty Aluminum Foil
- **¼** cup honey
- **2** tablespoons Dijon mustard
- **1½** tablespoons melted butter or olive oil
- **2** teaspoons Worcestershire sauce
- **1** tablespoon cornstarch
- **⅛** teaspoon white pepper (optional)
- **1** pound fresh or frozen asparagus spears
- **4** salmon fillets or steaks (4 to 6 ounces *each*)
- **⅓** cup chopped walnuts

PREHEAT grill to medium-high. Blend honey, mustard, butter, Worcestershire sauce, cornstarch and pepper; set aside.

CENTER one-fourth of asparagus on each sheet of Reynolds Wrap Heavy Duty Aluminum Foil. Top with salmon fillets; drizzle with reserved honey-mustard sauce. Sprinkle with walnuts.

BRING up foil sides. Double fold top and ends to seal packet, leaving room for heat circulation inside. Repeat to make four packets.

GRILL 9 to 11 minutes in covered grill.

Makes 4 servings

Oriental Vegetable Packet

Prep Time: 12 minutes ● **Grill Time:** 10 minutes

- 1 **sheet (18×24 inches) Reynolds Wrap® Heavy Duty Aluminum Foil**
- 2 **cups broccoli florets**
- 2 **cups snow peas**
- 1 **medium onion, sliced**
- 1 **medium red bell pepper, cut into strips**
- 2 **tablespoons soy sauce**
- 2 **cloves garlic, minced**
- 1 **tablespoon vegetable oil or sesame oil**
- ½ **teaspoon minced fresh ginger (optional)**
- ¼ **teaspoon crushed red pepper flakes (optional)**

PREHEAT grill to medium-high.

CENTER vegetables on sheet of Reynolds Wrap Heavy Duty Aluminum Foil. Top with soy sauce, garlic and oil. Sprinkle with ginger and red pepper flakes, if desired.

BRING up foil sides. Double fold top and ends to seal making one large foil packet, leaving room for heat circulation inside.

GRILL 10 to 12 minutes in covered grill.

Makes 4 to 6 servings

Pepper Steak with Black Beans Packets

Prep Time: 10 minutes • **Grill Time:** 9 minutes

- **4** sheets (12×18 inches *each*) Reynolds Wrap® Heavy Duty Aluminum Foil
- **1** pound boneless beef sirloin steak, ½-inch thick
- **2** cups frozen yellow, green and red peppers with onions
- **1** can (15 ounces) black beans, rinsed and drained
- **1** cup liquid fajita marinade
  Flour tortillas
- **1** cup shredded Cheddar cheese for tacos

PREHEAT grill to medium-high. Cut steak lengthwise in half and then crosswise into ⅛-inch-thick strips. Combine steak strips, peppers with onions, black beans and fajita marinade.

CENTER one-fourth of steak mixture on each sheet of Reynolds Wrap Heavy Duty Aluminum Foil.

BRING up foil sides. Double fold top and ends to seal packet, leaving room for heat circulation inside. Repeat to make four packets.

GRILL 9 to 11 minutes in covered grill. Serve with tortillas; sprinkle with cheese before serving.

Makes 4 servings

REYNOLDS KITCHENS TIP:

Substitute 1 envelope (about 1.2 ounces) dry fajita seasoning mix for liquid marinade. Prepare following package directions.

Pesto Chicken and Vegetables Packets

Prep Time: 5 minutes ● **Grill Time:** 10 minutes

- **2** sheets (12×18 inches *each*) Reynolds Wrap® Heavy Duty Aluminum Foil
- **2** boneless, skinless chicken breast halves (4 to 6 ounces *each*)
- **¼** cup prepared pesto sauce, divided
- **1** medium zucchini, sliced
- **4** red bell pepper rings, ¼-inch thick
  Salt and pepper to taste

PREHEAT grill to medium-high.

PLACE one chicken breast half on each sheet of Reynolds Wrap Heavy Duty Aluminum Foil.

SPREAD a thin layer of pesto sauce over chicken. Arrange vegetables beside chicken. Top with remaining pesto sauce. Sprinkle with salt and pepper.

BRING up foil sides. Double fold top and ends to seal packet, leaving room for heat circulation inside. Repeat to make two packets.

GRILL 10 to 12 minutes in covered grill.

Makes 2 servings

Cheese Steak Packets

Prep Time: 10 minutes ● **Grill Time:** 8 minutes

- **4** sheets (12×18-inches *each*) Reynolds Wrap® Release® Non-Stick Foil
- **1** pound boneless beef sirloin steak, ½-inch thick
  Salt and pepper to taste
- **2** medium onions, thinly sliced
- **1** cup shredded Cheddar cheese
- **4** sub or hoagie-style buns
  Ketchup or steak sauce

PREHEAT grill to medium-high. Cut steak lengthwise in half; then crosswise into ⅛-inch thick strips. Sprinkle steak strips with salt and pepper; set aside.

CENTER one-fourth of onions on each sheet of Reynolds Wrap Release Non-Stick Foil. Top with steak strips and cheese.

BRING up foil sides. Double fold top and ends to seal packet, leaving room for heat circulation inside. Repeat to make four packets.

GRILL 8 to 10 minutes in covered grill. Serve on sliced buns with additional cheese, if desired. Top with ketchup or steak sauce.

Makes 4 servings

Turkey Burrito Packets

Prep Time: 10 minutes ● **Grill Time:** 18 minutes

- **4** sheets (12×18 inches *each*) Reynolds Wrap® Release® Non-Stick Foil
- **4** (8-inch) flour tortillas
- **½** pound ground turkey
- **1** can (9 ounces) bean dip
- **1** cup shredded Cheddar cheese
- **¼** cup chopped onion
- **¼** cup chunky salsa
- Sour cream, chopped fresh cilantro

PREHEAT grill to medium-high indirect heat. For indirect heat, the heat source (coals or gas burner) is on one side of grill. Place foil packets on opposite side with no coals or flame underneath.

CENTER one tortilla on each sheet of Reynolds Wrap Release Non-Stick Foil with non-stick (dull) side toward food. Combine turkey, bean dip, cheese, onion and salsa. Spoon mixture onto tortillas. Wrap filling in each tortilla, burrito-style; place seam-side down.

BRING up foil sides. Double fold top and ends to seal packet, leaving room for heat circulation inside. Repeat to make four packets.

GRILL 18 to 20 minutes in covered grill. Serve with sour cream and cilantro.

Makes 4 servings

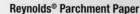

Apple Galette

Prep Time: 25 minutes ● **Cook Time:** 35 minutes

Reynolds® Parchment Paper
5 Granny Smith Apples (about 2 pounds), peeled, cored and thinly sliced
¾ cup packed light brown sugar
2 tablespoons flour
1 teaspoon ground cinnamon
¼ teaspoon ground nutmeg
1 refrigerated pie crust (15-ounce package) OR your favorite 1 crust recipe
¼ cup chopped pecans
1 tablespoon butter, cut into small pieces
2 teaspoons milk
Granulated sugar

PREHEAT oven to 400°F. Place a 14-inch sheet of Reynolds Parchment Paper on counter; sprinkle lightly with flour. Center piecrust dough on parchment; roll into a 12-inch circle.

COMBINE apples, brown sugar, flour, cinnamon and nutmeg in large bowl; set aside. Spoon apple filling into center of dough, leaving a 2-inch border uncovered. Sprinkle filling with pecans; top with butter. Use parchment paper to lift pie crust border up over filling, pleating edges and leaving an opening in center.

PLACE Galette on parchment paper onto a cookie sheet with sides. Press dough together to seal any cracks to prevent juices from leaking during baking. Brush dough lightly with milk; sprinkle with sugar.

BAKE 30 minutes or until crust is golden brown. Cover Galette with Reynolds Wrap® Aluminum Foil to prevent over browning. Continue baking 5 to 10 minutes longer until juices bubble and apples are tender. Cool 15 minutes. Serve warm, if desired.

Makes 8 servings

REYNOLDS KITCHENS TIPS:

Be sure to use a cookie sheet with sides. This will prevent any juices that might leak during baking from dripping onto your oven.

Golden Delicious apples are a great substitute for this recipe.

Mixed Apple Salad with Creamy Orange Dressing

Prep Time: 20 minutes ● **Chill Time:** 1 hour

Reynolds® Plastic Wrap
- ⅓ cup orange marmalade
- 2 tablespoons apple juice
- 2 tablespoons fresh lemon juice
- 5 to 6 large apples with different color peels, each sliced into 8 to 12 wedges
- ⅓ cup sweetened dried cranberries

CREAMY ORANGE DRESSING
- 3 ounces cream cheese, softened
- ⅓ cup orange marmalade
- 1 container (6 ounces) vanilla yogurt
- 2 teaspoons fresh lemon juice

GLAZED PECANS (optional)
- ½ cup pecan pieces
- 2 tablespoons sugar

MIX orange marmalade, apple juice and lemon juice in large glass serving bowl until smooth. Add sliced apples and dried cranberries to bowl; toss gently to coat apples. Cover bowl with a sheet of Reynolds Plastic Wrap. Refrigerate until ready to serve.

BEAT cream cheese and orange marmalade in small bowl on medium speed with electric mixer until smooth. Add yogurt and lemon juice; beat until smooth. Pour dressing into small glass bowl; cover bowl with plastic wrap. Refrigerate 1 hour or until chilled.

MAKE GLAZED PECANS, if desired. Place pecans and sugar in small skillet. Stir constantly over medium heat until sugar melts and coats pecans. Spread pecans on sheet of Reynolds Wrap® Release® Non-Stick Foil; cool completely. Sprinkle Glazed Pecans over apple salad just before serving.

Makes 8 to 10 servings

Chocolate Raspberry Mousse

Prep Time: 10 minutes ● **Chill Time:** 3 hours

Reynolds® Plastic Wrap

10 chocolate sandwich cookies, crushed (about 1 cup)

2 tablespoons butter or margarine, melted

1 package (3.9 ounces) instant chocolate pudding mix

¾ cup milk

1 container (12 ounces) frozen whipped topping, thawed, divided

¾ cup raspberry or strawberry jam

Milk chocolate candy bar shavings

Fresh raspberries or strawberries (optional)

COMBINE chocolate cookie crumbs and butter in a 1½-quart serving dish. Press into bottom of dish to form a crust; set aside.

WHISK chocolate pudding mix and milk together in large bowl. Stir in one-third of the whipped topping. Spoon mixture evenly over crust.

STIR jam until smooth in medium bowl; stir in remaining whipped topping. Spread evenly over pudding layer. Cover with Reynolds Plastic Wrap and refrigerate 3 hours or overnight.

SPRINKLE with chocolate shavings before serving. Garnish with fresh raspberries or strawberries, if desired.

Makes 6 to 8 servings

REYNOLDS KITCHENS TIPS:

*Place a sheet of Reynolds®
Cut-Rite® Wax Paper over
cookie crumbs to protect
hands when forming crust.*

*Use a vegetable peeler to make
chocolate candy bar shavings.*

Tropical Meringue Dessert Squares

Prep Time: 25 minutes ● **Cook Time:** 30 minutes

Reynolds® Parchment Paper

CRUST
- 1 cup flour
- ⅓ cup powdered sugar
- ½ cup (1 stick) butter, softened

LIME FILLING
- 1 cup sugar
- 6 tablespoons fresh or bottled key lime juice

- 6 large eggs, separated (reserve 3 egg whites for meringue)
- ¼ cup butter, softened

MERINGUE
- ½ teaspoon cream of tartar
- ⅓ cup sugar
- ⅓ cup sweetened flaked coconut

PREHEAT oven to 375°F. Line 9×9×2-inch baking pan with Reynolds Parchment Paper.

FOR CRUST: Combine flour, powdered sugar and butter until crumbly; press into parchment-lined pan. **BAKE** 15 minutes; remove from oven.

FOR LIME FILLING: While crust is baking, combine sugar, lime juice, 6 egg yolks and butter in medium saucepan. Cook over medium heat, whisking frequently until thickened, about 8 to 10 minutes; set aside.

FOR MERINGUE: Combine 3 reserved egg whites and cream of tartar in medium bowl (reserve remaining egg whites for another use). Beat on high speed with electric mixer until soft peaks form. Continue beating about 2 minutes, gradually adding sugar until stiff peaks form; set aside.

SPREAD lime filling evenly over crust. Spread meringue evenly over lime filling. Sprinkle coconut over meringue. Return to oven.

BAKE 10 to 13 minutes or until coconut is lightly browned. Remove from oven, cool completely. Use edges of parchment lining to lift dessert from pan. Place on cutting board. Pull back edges of parchment for easy cutting. Cut into 16 squares. Serve immediately or refrigerate.

Makes 16 servings

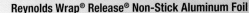

Chocolate Dessert Shells

Prep Time: 20 minutes ● **Chill Time:** 1 hour

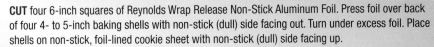

Reynolds Wrap® Release® Non-Stick Aluminum Foil
- ¾ cup semi-sweet chocolate chips
- 2 teaspoons shortening
- Orange or raspberry sherbet
- Vanilla ice cream

CUT four 6-inch squares of Reynolds Wrap Release Non-Stick Aluminum Foil. Press foil over back of four 4- to 5-inch baking shells with non-stick (dull) side facing out. Turn under excess foil. Place shells on non-stick, foil-lined cookie sheet with non-stick (dull) side facing up.

MICROWAVE chocolate and shortening in microwave-safe bowl on HIGH, 1 to 2 minutes, until chocolate is soft. Stir until smooth. Coat shells with chocolate; refrigerate at least 1 hour.

REMOVE baking shells carefully, leaving foil backing on chocolate shells. Peel foil from chocolate shells by placing chocolate side down on serving plate and gently peeling off foil.

FILL each shell with small scoops of sherbet and/or ice cream. Serve immediately.

Makes 4 servings

REYNOLDS KITCHENS TIPS:

Use the back of a spoon to carefully spread chocolate over back of non-stick foil-covered shells. (Do not spread over edge; this will cause chocolate to crack when removing baking shell.) Refrigerate 1 to 2 hours.

If chocolate begins to soften when you are removing the foil backing, refrigerate 30 to 60 minutes longer or until firm.

Mini Fruit Pizzas

Prep Time: 15 minutes ● Cook Time: 16 minutes

- **20 Reynolds® FunShapes™ Stars or Hearts Baking Cups**
- **1 package (18 ounces) refrigerated sugar cookie dough rounds**
- **1 package (8 ounces) cream cheese, softened**
- **¼ cup orange marmalade**
- **¼ cup powdered sugar**
- **Fresh fruit, sliced**

PREHEAT oven to 350°F. Place Reynolds FunShapes Stars or Hearts Baking Cups on two cookie sheets with sides; set aside.

PLACE one sugar cookie dough round in the center of each baking cup.

BAKE 16 to 21 minutes or until golden brown; cool. Remove cookies from baking cups.

MIX cream cheese, orange marmalade and powdered sugar in small bowl. Spread about ¼ cup mixture onto each cookie. Arrange fruit slices over cream cheese mixture. Cover with Reynolds® Plastic Wrap; refrigerate until ready to serve.

Makes 20 servings

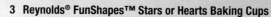

Prep Time: 10 minutes ● **Chill Time:** 2 hours

- **3 Reynolds® FunShapes™ Stars or Hearts Baking Cups**
- **1 package (8 ounces) cream cheese, softened**
- **1 tablespoon ranch salad dressing and seasoning mix**
  Assorted crackers and vegetables

PLACE Reynolds FunShapes Stars or Hearts Baking Cups on cookie sheet with sides. Spray baking cups with nonstick cooking spray; set aside.

MIX cream cheese and ranch seasoning mix in medium bowl until well blended.

SPOON 1/3 cup cream cheese mixture into each baking cup. Spread evenly with knife or small spatula.

COVER with Reynolds® Plastic Wrap; refrigerate 2 hours or until firm. Invert onto a serving platter. Serve with assorted crackers or vegetables.

Makes 9 to 10 servings

Smoked Salmon Spread

Prep Time: 10 minutes ● **Chill Time:** 2 hours

 3 Reynolds® FunShapes™ Stars or Hearts Baking Cups
 1 package (8 ounces) cream cheese, softened
 ½ cup smoked salmon, finely chopped
 1 teaspoon dried dill weed
  Assorted crackers

PLACE Reynolds FunShapes Stars or Hearts Baking Cups on cookie sheet with sides. Spray baking cups with nonstick cooking spray; set aside.

MIX cream cheese, salmon and dill weed in medium bowl until well blended.

SPOON ⅓ cup of cream cheese mixture into each baking cup. Spread evenly with knife or small spatula.

COVER with Reynolds® Plastic Wrap; refrigerate 2 hours or until firm. Invert onto a serving platter. Serve with assorted crackers.

Makes 9 to 10 servings

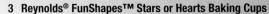

Prep Time: 10 minutes ● **Chill Time:** 2 hours

- 3 Reynolds® FunShapes™ Stars or Hearts Baking Cups
- 1 package (8 ounces) cream cheese, softened
- ½ cup finely chopped red, green and yellow bell peppers
- 2 teaspoons salt-free tomato basil garlic seasoning

  Assorted crackers and vegetables

PLACE Reynolds FunShapes Stars or Hearts Baking Cups on cookie sheet with sides. Spray baking cups with nonstick cooking spray; set aside.

MIX cream cheese, peppers and seasoning in medium bowl until well blended.

SPOON ⅓ cup cream cheese mixture into each baking cup. Spread evenly with knife or small spatula.

COVER with Reynolds® Plastic Wrap; refrigerate 2 hours or until firm. Invert onto a serving platter. Serve with assorted crackers and vegetables.

Makes 9 to 10 servings

Asparagus Packet with Mustard Sauce

Prep Time: 10 minutes ● **Cook Time:** 14 minutes

- 1 sheet (18×24 inches) Reynolds Wrap® Heavy Duty Aluminum Foil
- 2 pounds fresh asparagus, trimmed
- 3 tablespoons olive oil or butter
- Salt and pepper to taste

SAUCE

- 1 cup light sour cream
- 2 tablespoons red wine vinegar
- ¼ cup Dijon mustard
- 2 teaspoons sugar
- ⅛ teaspoon crushed red pepper

PREHEAT oven to 450°F OR grill to medium-high.

CENTER asparagus on sheet of Reynolds Wrap Heavy Duty Aluminum Foil; top with olive oil.

BRING up foil sides. Double fold top and ends to seal making one large foil packet, leaving room for heat circulation inside.

BAKE 14 to 16 minutes on cookie sheet in oven **OR GRILL** 7 to 9 minutes in covered grill. Open foil; season with salt and pepper.

COMBINE sour cream, vinegar, mustard, sugar and red pepper in small microwave-safe bowl to make sauce. Microwave on HIGH 1½ to 2 minutes or until warm, stir. Serve sauce over asparagus.

Makes 6 to 8 servings

Herbed Green Beans with Roasted Peppers Packet

Prep Time: 20 minutes • **Cook Time:** 30 minutes

- 1 sheet (18×24 inches) Reynolds Wrap® Aluminum Foil
- 2 pounds whole green beans, trimmed OR 2 packages (16 ounces *each*) frozen whole green beans
- 1 jar (7 ounces) roasted red peppers, drained and cut into strips
- ¼ cup French fried onions, crushed
- 2 tablespoons water
- 1 tablespoon olive oil or butter
- 2 teaspoons dried basil
- ¾ teaspoon salt
- ⅛ teaspoon pepper

PREHEAT oven to 450°F OR grill to medium-high.

CENTER green beans on sheet of Reynolds Wrap Aluminum Foil with non-stick (dull) side toward food. Top with roasted red peppers, French fried onions, water, olive oil, basil, salt and pepper.

BRING up foil sides. Double fold top and ends to form one large foil packet, leaving room for heat circulation inside.

BAKE 30 to 35 minutes on cookie sheet in oven **OR GRILL** 15 to 20 minutes in covered grill. Sprinkle with additional French fried onions before serving, if desired.

Makes 8 to 10 servings

REYNOLDS KITCHENS TIP:

If using frozen green beans, increase baking time to 35 to 40 minutes or grilling time to 20 to 25 minutes.

Roasted Boneless Leg of Lamb

Prep Time: 10 minutes ● **Cook Time:** 1½ hours

- 1 Reynolds® Oven Bag, Large Size
- 1 tablespoon flour
- 1 (4- to 5-pound) boneless leg of lamb
- 1 tablespoon olive oil
- 4 cloves garlic, minced
- 2 teaspoons dried thyme
- 1 teaspoon dried rosemary
- 1 teaspoon salt
- ½ teaspoon pepper

PREHEAT oven to 325°F.

SHAKE flour in Reynolds Oven Bag; place in roasting pan at least 2 inches deep.

TRIM fat from lamb, leaving a thin layer. Brush both sides of lamb with oil. Combine garlic, thyme, rosemary, salt and pepper in small bowl. Rub lamb with herb mixture. Place lamb in oven bag.

CLOSE oven bag with nylon tie; cut six ½-inch slits in top. Insert meat thermometer through slit in oven bag into thickest part of lamb. Tuck ends of bag into pan.

BAKE 1½ to 2 hours or until meat thermometer reads 150°F for medium-rare or 160°F for medium. Let stand in oven bag 15 minutes.

Makes 16 to 20 servings

Orange Basil Roast Chicken

Prep Time: 10 minutes ● Cook Time: 1 1/4 hours

1 **Reynolds® Oven Bag, Large Size**
1 **tablespoon flour**
1 **(5- to 7-pound) whole roasting chicken**
8 **large fresh basil leaves**
1 **large orange, thinly sliced, divided**
1 **medium onion, sliced**
  Vegetable or olive oil
1 **teaspoon freshly ground black pepper**

PREHEAT oven to 350°F.

SHAKE flour in Reynolds Oven Bag; place in 13×9×2-inch baking pan.

LOOSEN skin of chicken over breast area by slipping your fingers or a knife under the skin. Place basil leaves and 4 orange slices under the skin. Divide onion slices and remaining orange slices between cavity of chicken and bottom of oven bag. Tuck the wings under the chicken and tie legs together, if desired. Brush chicken with oil; sprinkle with pepper. Place chicken in bag on top of onion and orange slices.

CLOSE oven bag with nylon tie; cut six 1/2-inch slits in top.

BAKE 1 1/4 to 1 1/2 hours, until chicken is tender and meat thermometer reads 180°F. For easy slicing, let stand in oven bag 10 minutes.

Makes 9 to 12 (3-ounce) servings

Ham with Peach Sauce

Prep Time: 10 minutes ● **Cook Time:** 1¼ hours

- 1 Reynolds® Oven Bag, Large Size
- ¼ cup flour
- 2 cans (29 ounces *each*) sliced peaches in heavy syrup, drained
- 1 cup peach or apricot preserves
- 1½ teaspoons ground cinnamon
- 1 (6- to 8-pound) boneless fully cooked ham
   Whole cloves (optional)

PREHEAT oven to 325°F.

SHAKE flour in Reynolds Oven Bag; place in 13×9×2-inch baking pan.

ADD peaches, peach preserves and cinnamon to oven bag. Squeeze bag to blend in flour. Arrange ingredients in an even layer in bag. Using a sharp knife, lightly score surface of ham in a diamond pattern. Insert cloves in the diamonds, if desired. Place ham in bag.

CLOSE oven bag with nylon tie; cut six ½-inch slits in top.

BAKE 1¼ to 1¾ hours or until meat thermometer reads 140°F. To serve, cut open oven bag, transfer ham to serving platter. Spoon sauce over ham.

Makes 24 to 32 (3-ounce) servings

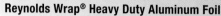

Apple Stuffed Pork Chops

Prep Time: 15 minutes ● **Cook Time:** 23 minutes

Reynolds Wrap® Heavy Duty Aluminum Foil
- 4 boneless center cut pork chops, 1¼-inch thick
- 1 package (6 ounces) stuffing mix for pork
- ½ cup chopped apple
- ¼ cup dried sweetened cranberries
- ½ teaspoon seasoned salt
- ¼ teaspoon pepper
- 2 tablespoons packed brown sugar
- 1 tablespoon butter, melted

PREHEAT oven to 425°F. For easy cleanup, line 10×15×1-inch pan with Reynolds Wrap Heavy Duty Aluminum Foil. (For quickest way to line a pan, see tip on page 5.)

CUT a pocket in each pork chop with sharp knife. Prepare stuffing mix following package directions. Stir in apple and cranberries; set aside.

PLACE chops in foil-lined pan; sprinkle with seasoned salt and pepper. Stuff each chop with ½ cup stuffing. Press to flatten.

BAKE 18 to 20 minutes. Remove from oven. **HEAT BROILER.** Mix brown sugar and butter; brush onto chops. Broil 3 to 4 inches from heat 5 to 8 minutes or until brown.

Makes 4 servings

Baked Fiesta Enchiladas

Prep Time: 25 minutes ● **Cook Time:** 20 minutes

Reynolds Wrap® Release® Non-Stick Foil
1   medium red bell pepper, chopped
1   package (8 ounces) sliced fresh mushrooms
½   cup sliced green onions
1   tablespoon vegetable or olive oil
1   cup sour cream
1   can (10¾ ounces) cream of chicken soup, undiluted
1   package (8 ounces) shredded sharp Cheddar cheese, divided
1   jar (2½ ounces) sliced ripe olives, drained (optional)
2   cups chopped cooked chicken or turkey
6   (8- to 10-inch) spinach, tomato or flour tortillas
1   jar (16 ounces) salsa
Chopped fresh cilantro (optional)

PREHEAT oven to 350°F. For easy cleanup, line 13×9×2-inch baking pan with Reynolds Wrap Release Non-Stick Foil with non-stick (dull) side toward food; set aside. (For tip, see page 5.)

COMBINE red pepper, mushrooms, onions and oil in medium saucepan. Over medium-high heat, stir and cook until pepper and mushrooms are tender; drain. Add sour cream, soup, half of cheese and olives. Stir in chicken.

SPOON about ¾ to 1 cup filling down center of tortillas, roll up and place side by side in foil-lined pan. Top with salsa and remaining cheese.

BAKE 20 to 25 minutes or until thoroughly heated. Top with sour cream and chopped fresh cilantro, if desired.

Makes 6 servings

Baked Ziti

Prep Time: 20 minutes ● **Cook Time:** 1 hour

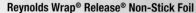

Reynolds Wrap® Release® Non-Stick Foil

1	**pound ground beef, browned and drained**
4	**cups (about a 32 ounce jar) chunky garden-style pasta sauce**
1	**tablespoon Italian seasoning, divided**
1	**package (16 ounces) ziti pasta, cooked and drained**
1	**package (8 ounces) shredded mozzarella cheese, divided**
1	**container (15 ounces) ricotta cheese OR cottage cheese**
1	**egg**
¼	**cup grated Parmesan cheese, divided**

PREHEAT oven to 350°F.

COMBINE ground beef, pasta sauce and 2 teaspoons Italian seasoning. Stir pasta into meat sauce; spread half of mixture evenly in pan. Top with half of mozzarella cheese.

COMBINE ricotta cheese, egg, 2 tablespoons Parmesan cheese and remaining Italian seasoning; spread over mozzarella cheese in pan. Spread remaining pasta mixture over ricotta cheese mixture. Sprinkle with remaining mozzarella and Parmesan cheeses.

COVER with Reynolds Wrap Release Non-Stick Foil with non-stick (dull) side toward food.

BAKE 45 minutes. Remove foil cover and **CONTINUE BAKING** 15 minutes or until cheese is melted and lightly browned. Let stand 15 minutes before serving.

Makes 8 servings

Slow Cooker Pot Roast

Prep Time: 15 minutes ● **Cook Time:** 8 hours

- **1 Reynolds® Slow Cooker Liner**
- **¼ cup water**
- **4 medium red potatoes, cut in quarters**
- **1 medium onion, cut in quarters**
- **1 package (16 ounces) peeled baby carrots**
- **1 envelope (1 ounce) onion soup mix, divided**
- **¼ teaspoon *each* salt, pepper and dried thyme**
- **2½ to 3 pound boneless beef chuck pot roast**

OPEN slow cooker liner and place it inside a 5- to 6½-quart slow cooker bowl. Fit liner snugly against the bottom and sides of bowl; pull top of liner over rim of bowl.

PLACE water and three-fourths of the vegetables in lined-slow cooker. Reserve 1 tablespoon onion soup mix. Sprinkle remaining onion soup mix over vegetables; stir gently to coat evenly. Sprinkle and rub salt, pepper and thyme over pot roast. Place pot roast on top of vegetables. Place remaining vegetables around pot roast; sprinkle vegetables with remaining onion soup mix. Place lid on slow cooker.

COOK on LOW for 8 to 9 hours OR on HIGH for 5 to 6 hours or until pot roast is tender.

CAREFULLY remove lid to allow steam to escape. Serve food directly from slow cooker. Do not lift or transport liner with food inside. Cool slow cooker completely; remove liner and toss.

Makes 6 to 8 (3-ounce) servings

REYNOLDS KITCHENS TIP:

If desired, substitute four peeled white potatoes for red potatoes AND substitute four whole carrots, peeled and cut in 2-inch pieces for peeled baby carrots.

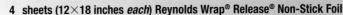

Baked Fish with Almond Couscous Packets

Prep Time: 15 minutes ● **Cook Time:** 20 minutes

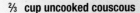

- **4** sheets (12×18 inches *each*) Reynolds Wrap® Release® Non-Stick Foil
- **⅔** cup uncooked couscous
- **¼** cup sliced green onion
- **1** teaspoon ground coriander
- **¾** teaspoon paprika
- **¼** teaspoon hot pepper sauce
- **½** cup sliced almonds
- **½** cup currants
- **1** can (10½ ounces) double strength chicken broth, divided
- **4** cod, flounder or halibut fillets (4 to 6 ounces *each*)
- **2** tablespoons melted butter or olive oil
- **1** lemon, thinly sliced
- **2** tablespoons chopped fresh parsley

PREHEAT oven to 450°F or grill to medium-high. Combine first 7 ingredients. Stir in half of chicken broth.

CENTER one-fourth of the mixture on each sheet of Reynolds Wrap Release Non-Stick Foil with non-stick (dull) side toward food. Top with fish fillet, butter and lemon slices.

BRING up foil sides. Double fold top and one end of packet. Through open end, add one-fourth of remaining chicken broth. Double fold remaining end to seal packet, leaving room for heat circulation inside. Repeat to make four packets.

BAKE 20 to 25 minutes on a cookie sheet in oven **OR GRILL** 8 to 10 minutes in covered grill. Sprinkle with parsley before serving.

Makes 4 servings

REYNOLDS KITCHENS TIP:

A pound of scallops may be substituted for the fish fillets.

Barbecue Chicken Packets

Prep Time: 10 minutes ● **Cook Time:** 18 minutes

- **4** sheets (12×18 inches *each*) Reynolds Wrap® Heavy Duty Aluminum Foil
- **4** boneless, skinless chicken breast halves (4 to 6 ounces each)
- **1** cup barbecue sauce
- **1** package (10 ounces) frozen whole kernel corn, OR 1 can (15¼ ounces) whole kernel corn, drained
- **½** cup chopped green bell pepper

PREHEAT oven to 450°F or grill to medium-high.

CENTER one chicken breast half on each sheet of Reynolds Wrap Heavy Duty Aluminum Foil. Spoon barbecue sauce over chicken. Top with vegetables.

BRING up foil sides. Double fold top and ends to seal packet, leaving room for heat circulation inside. Repeat to make four packets.

BAKE 18 to 22 minutes on cookie sheet in oven **OR GRILL** 12 to 15 minutes in covered grill.

Makes 4 servings

Caramel Cream Dessert

Prep Time: 15 minutes ● **Chill Time:** 2 hours

Reynolds® Color Plastic Wrap

- 1 **package (3 ounces) cream cheese, softened**
- 2 **cups frozen whipped topping, thawed**
- 1 **jar (12¼ ounces) caramel ice cream topping, divided**
- 2 **cups cubed pound cake**
- ¼ **cup chopped pecans, divided**
- 4 **to 6 medium fresh peaches, peeled and sliced OR 2 cans (15 ounces each) sliced peaches in juice, drained**
- ½ **pint fresh raspberries or strawberries**

BEAT cream cheese with an electric mixer in medium bowl until smooth. Add whipped topping and ¾ cup caramel ice cream topping. Beat until well blended; set aside.

PLACE pound cake cubes in 1½-quart serving bowl. Drizzle with ¼ cup caramel ice cream topping. Spread evenly with half of cream cheese mixture. Sprinkle with 2 tablespoons chopped pecans. Top with all the peaches and half the raspberries. Spread remaining cream cheese mixture over fruit. Sprinkle with remaining pecans and raspberries.

COVER with Reynolds Color Plastic Wrap and refrigerate at least 2 hours or overnight.

Makes 6 to 8 servings

REYNOLDS KITCHENS TIP:

To decorate bowl, fold a long sheet of Reynolds Color Plastic Wrap into a 2-inch wide strip. Wrap the strip of plastic wrap around the top edge of the bowl, overlapping ends. Tape end in place with double-sided tape.

Caribbean Jerk Chicken Packets

Prep Time: 10 minutes ● **Cook Time:** 20 minutes

- **4** sheets (12×18 inches *each*) Reynolds Wrap® Release® Non-Stick Foil
- **2** cups cooked rice
- **1** can (16 ounces) red beans or light red kidney beans, rinsed and drained
- **½** cup Caribbean jerk marinade, divided
- **4** boneless, skinless chicken breast halves (1 to 1¼ pounds)

PREHEAT oven to 450°F or grill to medium-high. Combine rice, beans and ¼ cup marinade.

CENTER one-fourth of mixture on each sheet of Reynolds Wrap Release Non-Stick Foil with non-stick (dull) side toward food. Top with chicken; drizzle with remaining marinade.

BRING up foil sides. Double fold top and ends to seal packet, leaving room for heat circulation inside. Repeat to make four packets.

BAKE 20 to 24 minutes on cookie sheet in oven OR GRILL 16 to 20 minutes in covered grill.

Makes 4 servings

Cherry Macadamia Oatmeal Cookies

Prep Time: 20 minutes ● **Cook Time:** 10 minutes

COOKIE

Reynolds® Parchment Paper
- 1¾ cups flour
- 1 teaspoon baking soda
- ½ teaspoon salt
- 1¼ cups packed brown sugar
- 1 cup (2 sticks) butter, softened
- ½ cup sugar
- 2 eggs
- 2 tablespoons milk
- 2 teaspoons vanilla extract
- 2½ cups quick oats, uncooked
- 1 package (12 ounces) semi-sweet chocolate chunks
- 1 cup coarsely chopped macadamia nuts
- ½ cup maraschino cherries, drained and quartered

ICING
- 1 cup powdered sugar
- 2 to 3 tablespoons water

PREHEAT oven to 375°F. Line 2 cookie sheets with Reynolds Parchment Paper; set aside.

COMBINE flour, baking soda and salt on another sheet of parchment paper; set aside.

BEAT brown sugar, butter and sugar together in large bowl, with an electric mixer 2 to 3 minutes or until light and fluffy. Beat in eggs, milk and vanilla. Reduce speed to low. Use parchment paper like a funnel to gradually add flour mixture to butter mixture, mixing well after each addition. Beat until well blended.

STIR in oats, chocolate chunks, nuts and cherries until well blended. Drop by rounded tablespoons 2 inches apart onto parchment-lined cookie sheets.

BAKE 10 to 12 minutes or until golden brown. Slide parchment paper with cookies onto a wire rack to cool. **FOR ICING,** stir together powdered sugar and water in small bowl. Drizzle over cooled cookies on parchment paper.

Makes 2 to 3 dozen cookies

REYNOLDS KITCHENS TIP:

Dry cherries well with paper towels to prevent the cherry juice from adding a pink color to dough.

Spicy Salmon with Pepper-Jack Rice Packets

Prep Time: 15 minutes ● **Cook Time:** 20 minutes

- **4** sheets (12×18-inches *each*) Reynolds Wrap® Release® Non-Stick Aluminum Foil
- **8** ounces Pepper-Jack cheese, shredded
- **¾** cup reduced-fat sour cream
- **½** cup water
- **1½** cups instant rice, uncooked
- **1** can (4 ounces) diced green chilies, drained
- **4** salmon steaks or fillets (4 to 6 ounces *each*)
- **½** fresh lime
- **½** teaspoon salt
- **½** teaspoon ground cumin
- **¼** teaspoon chili powder
- **⅛** teaspoon red pepper flakes (optional)

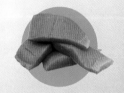

PREHEAT oven to 450°F.

COMBINE cheese, sour cream, and water. Stir in instant rice and green chilies.

ARRANGE one-fourth of rice mixture on non-stick (dull) side of each sheet of Reynolds Wrap Release Non-Stick Foil. Place a salmon fillet over each rice mound and press slightly to level rice. Squeeze lime over salmon.

COMBINE salt, cumin, chili powder and red pepper flakes. Sprinkle over salmon.

BRING up foil sides. Double fold top and ends to seal packet, leaving room for heat circulation inside. Repeat to make four packets.

BAKE 20 to 25 minutes on cookie sheet in oven.

Makes 4 servings

Prep Time: 15 minutes ● **Cook Time:** 30 minutes

- 1 Reynolds® Oven Bag, Large Size
- 1 tablespoon flour
- 1 jar (about 26 ounces) pasta sauce, divided
- 1 pound ground beef
- ½ small red bell pepper, finely chopped
- ¼ cup bread crumbs
- 1 egg
- 1½ teaspoon dried Italian seasoning
- 1 teaspoon salt
- 1 teaspoon garlic powder
- Hot cooked pasta or hoagie rolls (optional)
- Shredded Parmesan cheese (optional)

PREHEAT oven to 350°F.

SHAKE flour in Reynolds Oven Bag; place bag in 13×9×2-inch or larger baking pan at least 2 inches deep. Pour ⅔ cup pasta sauce in large bowl. Add remaining pasta sauce to bag; squeeze bag to blend in flour.

ADD remaining ingredients, except cooked pasta and Parmesan cheese, to pasta sauce in bowl; mix until well blended. Shape ground beef mixture into large meatballs, using about ⅓ cup for each meatball. Place meatballs in an even layer in oven bag.

CLOSE oven bag with nylon tie; cut six ½-inch slits in top. Tuck ends of bag in pan.

BAKE 30 minutes or until meat thermometer reads 160°F. Serve Super Italian Meatballs and sauce over hot cooked pasta OR cut in half and serve on hoagie rolls as meatball subs. Sprinkle shredded Parmesan cheese over meatballs, if desired.

Make 8 or 9 servings

REYNOLDS KITCHENS TIP:

Because Reynolds Oven Bags hold in the natural juices, use lean and super lean ground beef, if you like. Your meatballs will be flavorful and juicy without the additional fat.

Microwave Shrimp & Ravioli

Prep Time: 15 minutes ● **Cook Time:** 4 minutes

Reynolds® Parchment Paper

- **1** package (9 ounces) uncooked fresh cheese ravioli
- **1** tablespoon butter or olive oil
- ½ teaspoon grated lemon peel
- ½ teaspoon dried basil
- **1** tablespoon lemon juice
- ½ pound peeled and deveined medium raw shrimp

PREPARE ravioli as directed on package. Rinse and drain; set aside.

COMBINE butter, lemon peel and basil in shallow 1½-quart microwave–safe dish.

MICROWAVE on HIGH 45 seconds to 1 minute, or until butter is melted.

ADD lemon juice. Mix well. Add ravioli and shrimp. Toss to coat. Cover dish with Reynolds Parchment Paper.

MICROWAVE on HIGH (100% power), stirring once, 3 to 4 minutes longer or until shrimp are opaque in center.

Makes 2 servings

Quick Italian Chicken

Prep Time: 10 minutes ● **Cook Time:** 25 minutes

- 1 Reynolds® Oven Bag, Large Size
- 2 tablespoons flour
- 1 jar (about 14 ounces) pasta sauce
- 4 boneless, skinless chicken breast halves (4 to 6 ounces *each*)
- 1 medium green bell pepper, coarsely chopped
- 1 package (8 ounces) spaghetti, cooked, drained

PREHEAT oven to 350°F.

SHAKE flour in Reynolds Oven Bag; place in 13×9×2-inch baking pan.

ADD pasta sauce to oven bag. Squeeze bag to blend in flour. Add chicken and green pepper to bag. Turn bag to coat chicken with sauce. Arrange chicken in an even layer in bag.

CLOSE oven bag with nylon tie; cut six ½-inch slits in top.

BAKE 25 to 30 minutes or until meat thermometer inserted in chicken reads 170°F. Serve over hot cooked spaghetti.

Makes 4 servings

REYNOLDS KITCHENS TIP:

For bone-in chicken breast halves, bake 35 to 40 minutes.